DISCOVERING SCIENCE

Hot And Cold

Rebecca Hunter

www.raintreepublishers.co.uk
Visit our website to find out more information about **Raintree** books.

To order:
☎ Phone 44 (0) 1865 888112
🖶 Send a fax to 44 (0) 1865 314091
💻 Visit the Raintree Bookshop at www.raintreepublishers.co.uk to browse our
catalogue and order online.

First published in Great Britain by Raintree,
Halley Court, Jordan Hill, Oxford
OX2 8EJ, part of Harcourt Education.

Raintree is a registered trademark of Harcourt
Education Ltd.

Produced for Raintree by Discovery Books Ltd
Design: Ian Winton
Editorial: Rebecca Hunter
Consultant: Jeremy Bloomfield
Commissioned photography: Chris Fairclough
Illustrations: Keith Williams, Pamela Goodchild
 and Stefan Chabluk
Production: Jonathan Smith

Originated by Dot Gradations Ltd
Printed and bound in China by South China
 Printing Company

ISBN 1 844 21568 7 (hardback)
07 06 05 04 03
10 9 8 7 6 5 4 3 2 1

ISBN 1 844 21575 X (paperback)
08 07 06 05 04
10 9 8 7 6 5 4 3 2 1

British Library Cataloguing in Publication Data
Hunter, Rebecca
Hot and Cold. – (Discovering Science)
536.5

A full catalogue record for this book is available from the
British Library.

Acknowledgements
The publishers would like to thank the following for
permission to reproduce photographs:
Bruce Coleman: page **13** bottom (Dr Eckart Pott), **14**, **21**,
27 (both), **28** bottom (Staffan Widstrand); Clearview
Stoves: page **17**; Chris Fairclough: page **9**, **10**, **12**
(bottom), **18**; gettyimages: page **4** (Mike Timo), **6** (Peter
Correz), **16** (Greg Pease), **25** top (David Hiser), bottom
(Kevin Schafer), **29** (J McDermott); Oxford Scientific
Films: page **26**; Science Photo Library: page **5** (Adam G
Sylvester), **7** (Tony Craddock), **8** (Martin Bond), **12**, top
(Chris Priest & Mark Clarke), **13** top (Tony Buxton), **20**
(NOAO), **28** top (Fuste-Raga, Jerrican).

Cover photograph of thermal image of hand reproduced
with permission of Science Photo Library.

The publishers would like to thank the following schools
for their help in providing equipment, models and
locations for photography sessions: Bedstone College,
Bucknell, Moor Park, Ludlow and Packwood Haugh,
Shrewsbury.

Every effort has been made to contact copyright holders
of any material reproduced in this book.
Any omissions will be rectified in subsequent printings if
notice is given to the publishers.

Any words appearing in the text in bold, **like
this**, are explained in the Glossary.

CONTENTS

WHAT IS HEAT?

You probably know that a cup of soup is hot and that snow is cold. You probably also know that if you leave that cup of soup outside it will get cold. If you put a snowball into an oven, it will heat up and melt. Why are these things hot or cold, and why do their **temperatures** change?

You need to dress up warmly to play outside on a cold, snowy day.

Lava from a volcano is one of the hottest things found on Earth.

particles

All things contain particles. Heat energy comes from the movement of these particles.

HEAT ENERGY

All things – solids, like this book, liquids, like the soup in your cup, and even gases, like the air around us – are made up of tiny **particles**. The particles are so tiny that we can not see them. These particles are constantly **vibrating**, or moving around. The energy produced by these moving particles is called heat. The faster the particles vibrate, the hotter something is.

HEAT UP, COOL DOWN

When you step out into the sunshine, you get hot. When you play in the snow, you get cold. Why do these things happen?

GAINING HEAT

Just like people, things gain heat when they are exposed to something hotter than they are. Heat energy always moves from something that has more heat, to something that has less heat – never the other way around. So when you leave your cup of soup outside, it gets cold because it loses heat to the outside air. The air becomes very slightly warmer.

When you are cold, you will try to warm up or gain heat. Think of the ways you might do this. You might stand in front of a fire, warm your hands on a cup of hot cocoa, or soak yourself in a hot bath.

▲ *Earth is warmed by heat from the Sun. This produces a climate that is warm enough for plants to grow and provide a food supply for animals and people.*

In each case, the heat will move from the hot object, the fireplace, the cup of cocoa, or the hot water in the bath, to the colder object – you. Your body gains heat, and you warm up.

FRICTION

Have you ever rubbed your hands together to warm them up? They get warm because heat energy is produced by rubbing things together. This is caused by **friction**.

The bushmen of the Kalahari can make fire using a stick. They twirl the stick very fast between their hands. This creates friction, which produces enough heat to set fire to wood shavings.

The friction between the moving parts in a machine can create huge amounts of heat. This can be dangerous. Oiling machine parts reduces friction, and less heat is produced.

These cogs are well-oiled to reduce friction.

CHEMICAL REACTIONS

Sometimes when two substances are mixed together heat is released. This is called a chemical reaction.

When you strike a match, friction produces enough heat to start the reaction between the material on the match head and the oxygen in the air. The chemical reaction produces both heat and light that is given off from the flame.

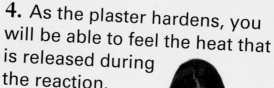

NEVER STRIKE MATCHES OR LIGHT FIRES UNLESS AN ADULT IS PRESENT.

PROJECT

You might like to do this simple and safe experiment to see how heat is produced in a chemical reaction.

You will need:
plaster of Paris
water
a tray of damp sand
a small object such as a shell or toy.

1. Press the object into the sand and then remove it leaving an impression.

2. Mix the plaster of Paris with water.

3. Pour the plaster of Paris into the impression in the sand.

4. As the plaster hardens, you will be able to feel the heat that is released during the reaction.

5. When the plaster is hard, you can remove the cast and paint your model.

How hot is it?

Temperature

We can tell how hot or cold something is by measuring its **temperature**. Temperature is measured with a **thermometer**.

The first thermometers were made using a glass tube. The glass tube was filled with a liquid metal called mercury. When the mercury in the thermometer was heated, it expanded, or took up more space, and was pushed up the tube. The more the mercury was heated, the further it moved up the tube. The temperature was read from a scale of degrees on the side of the thermometer.

It is important to serve food at the right temperature.

In winter it is cold. The mercury in the thermometer does not rise very far up the tube, so a low temperature shows. In the summer, as the temperature rises, the mercury rises further up the thermometer.

winter

FAHRENHEIT AND CELSIUS

The mercury thermometer we still use was invented in 1714 by German scientist Gabriel Fahrenheit. He named the scale of degrees after himself. On his scale water freezes at 32 degrees Fahrenheit (32 °F). Also on his scale, water boils at 212 degrees Fahrenheit (212 °F).

The human body temperature is 37 °C. Can you work out what this is in degrees Fahrenheit?

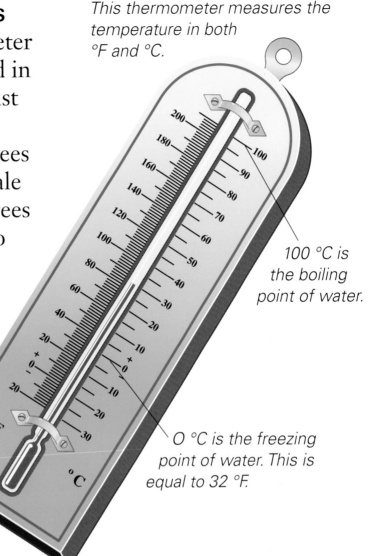

This thermometer measures the temperature in both °F and °C.

100 °C is the boiling point of water.

0 °C is the freezing point of water. This is equal to 32 °F.

summer

A few years later, Swedish professor Anders Celsius, invented a scale where 0 ° was the **freezing point** of water and 100 ° the **boiling point**. This was the Celsius scale (°C) that is usually used by scientists all over the world today.

THERMOMETERS TODAY

Today there are many different types of **thermometers**. Modern medical thermometers are usually electronic. These are used to measure the body **temperature** to check that a person is well.

STRIP THERMOMETERS

Strip thermometers are especially useful for measuring the temperature of small children and babies. The strip is pressed on to the child's forehead and changes colour according to his or her temperature.

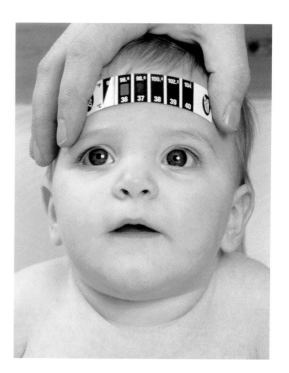

MAXIMUM AND MINIMUM THERMOMETERS

Weather forecasters and gardeners measure the air temperature outside with a thermometer that can record both the hottest and coldest times of the day. This thermometer is called a maximum and minimum thermometer. It has two tubes. The liquids in each tube move a marker that stays at the highest (maximum) or the lowest (minimum) temperature reached that day.

▲ The highest temperature ever recorded on Earth was in Africa, in the Sahara Desert. It was 58 °C (136 °F) in the shade.

◄ The coldest temperature ever recorded was -89 °C (-129 °F) at a weather station in Antarctica. This is much colder than inside your freezer at home, which is only -15 °C (5 °F)!

HEAT ON THE MOVE

Heat travels in three ways. These are called **convection, conduction** and **radiation**.

Eagles use thermals, or currents of air, to glide upwards.

CONVECTION

Have you ever watched a large bird soaring up into the sky without flapping its wings? How does a glider stay up in the air without an engine? The answer is that they are both riding **convection currents**. Heat travels through liquids and gases in convection currents.

The land is heated by the Sun. Heat from the land then heats the air above it. This causes tiny **particles** in the air to move around faster. The heated air becomes lighter and rises. Cooler, heavier air moves down to take its place. In this way, moving currents of air are created. This process is called convection. We call the upward currents of air **thermals**. It is these thermals that birds and gliders use to soar upwards.

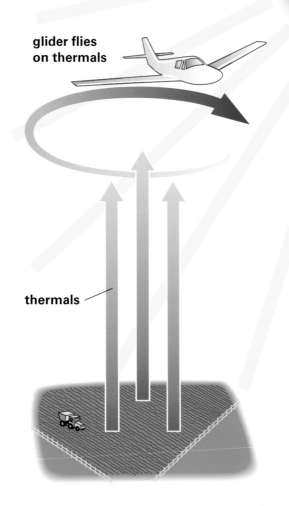

glider flies on thermals

thermals

Convection currents form as water is heated.

Heat also moves in this way through liquids. Every time you heat a kettle of water, a convection current forms in the kettle. The heated water rises from the bottom of the kettle while cooler water moves down to take its place. In this way, the heat is spread throughout the kettle until the **temperature** of all the water is the same.

CONDUCTION

Heat travels through solids in a different way. The **particles** in a solid do not move as freely as those in a liquid or a gas. When the particles in a solid are heated, they **vibrate** faster. They bump into each other, and pass their heat energy on to their neighbours. This transfer of heat is called **conduction**.

◄ *A blacksmith heats up an iron bar. The heat moves through the iron by conduction. When the bar is red-hot, the smith can bend it.*

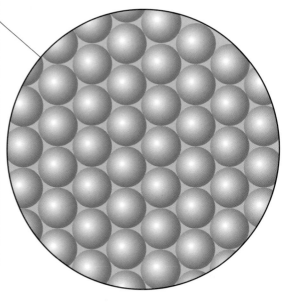

▲ *The particles in the cold metal are packed together closely and do not vibrate very much.*

◄ *As the metal is heated, the particles vibrate much faster. The heat is passed on to other particles and travels down the bar.*

Some solids allow heat to travel through them easily; others do not. Substances that allow heat to travel through them are called **thermal conductors**. Metals are the best thermal conductors. Saucepans, stoves and radiators are made of metal so they can heat up quickly.

This wood-burning stove is made of iron. Iron is a good conductor of heat, so the stove gives off lots of heat from the fire burning inside.

INSULATION

Substances that do not **conduct** heat well are called **insulators**. Insulators can be very useful in preventing heat transfer. Plastics, wood, cork, water, fibreglass and air are all poor **thermal conductors** and, therefore, good insulators.

Pot and pan handles are usually made of a special plastic, which means they stay cool. This means you can pick up a hot pan without getting burned.

PROJECT

This experiment shows the difference between conductors and insulators.

Stand with one bare foot on a tiled floor and one foot on a rug. The room is at the same **temperature** as both surfaces. However, one surface will feel cold and one warm.

This is because the tiles are good conductors of heat. They take heat away from your foot quickly, so they feel cold.

The rug is a poor conductor of heat. It takes very little heat away from your foot and leaves your foot feeling warm.

Insulators are also good for keeping heat in. We insulate our houses to keep them warm. Fibreglass in an attic stops heat from being lost upwards. Double or triple-glazed windows have layers of air sandwiched between panes of glass. This reduces the heat lost through the windows.

Fibreglass stops heat from being lost through the roof. Double glazing stops heat from being lost through the windows. Walls have insulation in them, too.

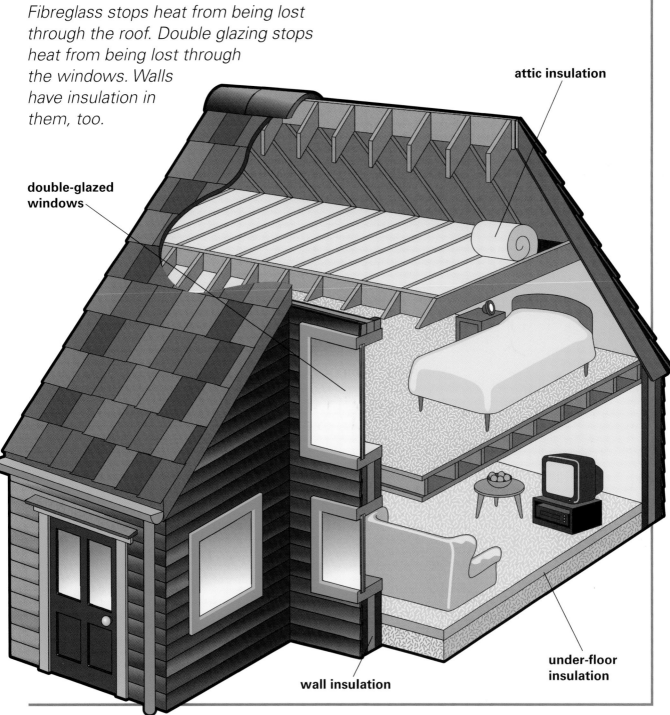

attic insulation

double-glazed windows

wall insulation

under-floor insulation

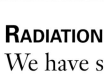

RADIATION

We have seen how heat can travel, making **particles** move faster in gases and liquids, by **convection** and through solids, by **conduction**. However, how does heat from the Sun move through space? There are no gases in space, no particles to move. The answer is that the Sun's heat, or energy, moves by **radiation**.

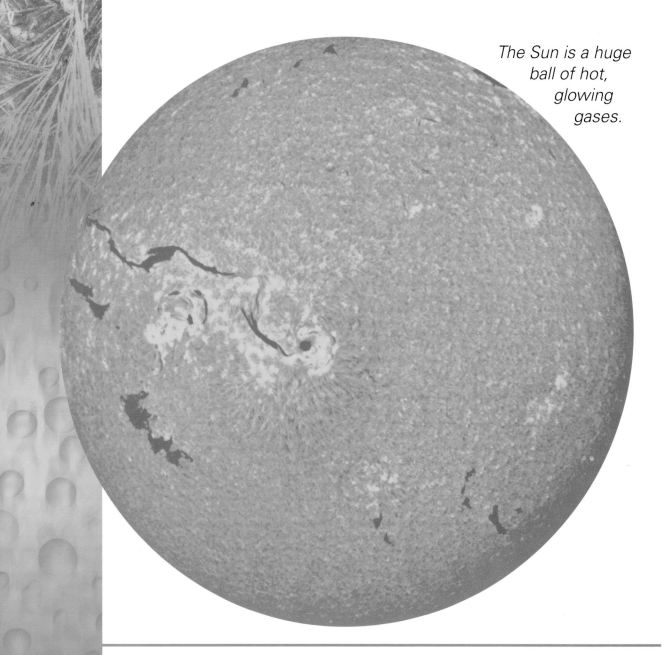

The Sun is a huge ball of hot, glowing gases.

All objects give out energy waves that travel through air and space. The movement of energy in waves is called radiation. Radiant energy does not need particles to help it move. Some radiant energy that reaches Earth is absorbed by the surface. This is how Earth is heated.

HEATING OUR EARTH

Energy from the Sun is carried to Earth by **radiation**. Some of this energy is changed to heat at the surface of Earth. Then Earth heats up the air in the atmosphere by **convection**. So why are **temperatures** not the same all over Earth? Why is it hotter at the **equator** than it is at the North and South Poles?

Earth receives heat from the Sun.

The Sun's rays heat the equator from directly above.

Away from the equator, the Sun's rays are spread over a larger area.

The temperature is different around the world because of the way the Sun's energy strikes the surface. Lands near the equator have high temperatures because the Sun is directly overhead. The Sun's energy centres on a smaller area, so these lands are hotter. At the North and South Poles, the Sun's rays strike Earth at an angle, so that the heat is spread over a bigger area. This makes temperatures much lower at the Poles.

PROJECT

This simple experiment illustrates the effect of the Sun on Earth's temperature.

1. Shine a torch directly onto a globe (below). The circle of light is small but bright.

2. Now shine the torch at an angle to the globe (above). The oval of light is larger but not as bright.

3. Can you see why the Sun's energy heats up the land around the equator more than the land around the Poles?

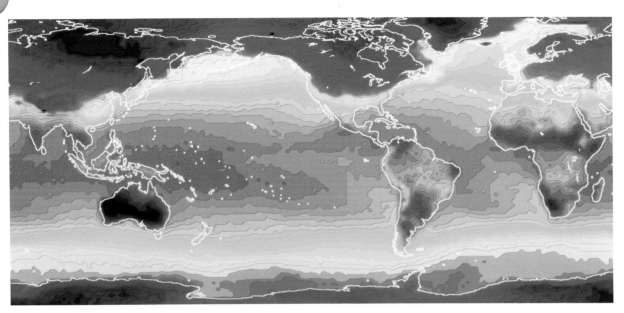

This picture shows the temperatures around the world in January. The hottest places are shown as red and the coldest are blue.

CLIMATE

The normal weather conditions in a place over a period of time are called that area's climate. Because Earth is heated more in some places than in others, different areas have different climates.

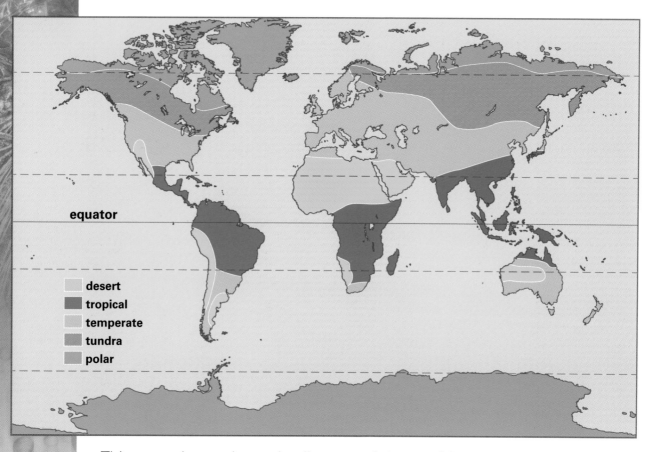

equator

desert
tropical
temperate
tundra
polar

This map shows the main climates of the world.

Lands near the equator are hot, and those near the Poles are cold – but climate does not just depend on where you are. Winds and ocean currents carry warmth around the world and affect the climate of the land. Distance from the ocean also affects the climate of a place, and so does its height above sea level. The higher a place is, the colder the climate is likely to be.

You can often guess the type of climate a country has by looking at the type of houses that are built there.

▶ *These igloos are the Inuit people's homes when they travel. They are built out of ice or snow and are very thick. The thick walls* **insulate** *the igloo and keep the heat inside.*

In Greece, where the climate is very warm, people often paint their houses white to reflect the sunlight and keep their houses cool. These houses also have thick walls to act as insulation and keep the heat out.

KEEP WARM, STAY COOL

All plants and animals need warmth to stay alive. Most plants stop growing when **temperatures** are below 6 °C (43 °F). Frosts can kill plants completely.

Different animals keep themselves warm in different ways. Animals that can control their own body temperature are called 'warm-blooded'. Animals with a body temperature that is controlled by their environment are called 'cold-blooded' (but this doesn't mean that their blood is cold).

WARM-BLOODED ANIMALS

Mammals, birds and humans are warm-blooded. Warm-blooded animals use several ways to control their body temperature. Many have an **insulating** layer of fat, plus fur or feathers to keep their body heat in.

Snow leopards are warm-blooded. They have thick, furry coats to keep them warm in the snow.

The food they eat is broken down inside their bodies and creates heat energy from inside.

A warm-blooded hummingbird spends all day searching for food and feeding.

If a warm-blooded animal gets too cold, its muscles will shiver. This movement produces some heat. If it gets too hot, it may sweat. When sweat **evaporates** from the skin, heat is taken away. The animal feels cooler.

COLD-BLOODED ANIMALS

Fish, reptiles and amphibians are cold-blooded animals. Cold-blooded animals control their body temperature through their behaviour. Lizards and snakes spend much of their time lying in the sun. This is to warm themselves up. Often they do not have the energy to feed or hunt unless their body is at the right temperature. When they get too hot, in the middle of the day for example, they have to find a cool spot in the shade to hide in and cool down.

A cold-blooded snake warms itself in the Australian sunshine.

CLOTHES FOR DIFFERENT CLIMATES

Humans have developed many ways of keeping warm. Our 'fur' is only a thin covering of hair, so we have to wear clothes to keep warm. The clothes help keep body heat from escaping into the air.

What we wear depends very much on the weather. When it is hot, we wear fewer clothes. We also wear light-coloured clothes that reflect the sunlight and keep us cooler.

◀ *A desert traveller wears loose, light-coloured clothing to stay cool.*

When it is cold, we wear more clothes made out of thicker fabrics that are good at **insulating** us against the weather.

▶ *These Inuit children look warm and happy in their thick jackets.*

CONTROLLING TEMPERATURE

Humans have learned how to keep warm by burning fuels and making electricity. We can now live in areas of the world where we would not have survived before. Electricity can also help us keep cool in hot places. Air conditioning, which removes heat from the air in a room or a car, allows people to live and travel in many of the hottest parts of the world.

Central heating and air conditioning mean we can control the temperature of our houses whatever the weather outside is.

GLOSSARY

boiling point temperature at which a liquid becomes a gas

conduction way that heat travels through solids

convection way that heat travels through liquids and gases

convection current current in air or a liquid that moves heat around

equator imaginary line around the middle of Earth

evaporate change of substance from a liquid to a gas

freezing point temperature at which a liquid becomes a solid

friction force between two things rubbing together

insulator material that stops heat from moving

particles tiny parts of a substance

radiation way heat travels through empty space

temperate lands with moderate temperatures that are not too hot or too cold

temperature measure of how hot or cold something is

thermal conductor material that allows heat to pass through it

thermals currents of rising warm air in the atmosphere

thermometer device that measures temperature

tundra lands on the edge of the polar regions that are bleak and treeless

vibration quick back-and-forth movement

FURTHER INFORMATION

BOOKS

Hot and Cold, Jack Challoner (Belitha Press, 2000)
Hot and Cold, Sally Hewitt (Franklin Watts, 2001)
Science all around me: Hot and Cold, Karen Bryant-Mole
(Heinemann Library, 1999)

WEBSITES

Animal Channel – video stories on animals and how to protect your pets
from the heat.
http://www.animalchannel.net

BBC Schools – information, games and activities on all aspects of science and
geography
http://www.bbc.co.uk/schools (select 'science' or 'geography')

Explore Science – access a library of information on many science topics.
Includes photos and artwork, video and animation, activities and tests.
http://www.heinemannexplore.com

Stanford Solar Center – games and activities about the Sun.
http://solar-center.stanford.edu

INDEX